1

A Bustle & Sew Publication

ISBN-13: 978-1512167504
ISBN-10: 1512167509

First published 2015 by:
Bustle & Sew
Coombe Leigh
Chillington
Kingsbridge
Devon TQ7 2LE
UK

www.bustleandsew.com

Welcome to the May Magazine .....

May is my most favourite month of the whole year as the countryside finally throws off all traces of its long winter slumber and bursts into life. All around is new life - delicate creamy-white hawthorn flowers festoon the hedgerows, cottage gardens are stuffed with tulips, bluebells and apple blossom and the jackdaws have returned to take up residence in the nesting boxes at the back of Coombe Leigh.

The lovely colours of spring are eagerly anticipated by us all, and appear all through this month's issue. As well as hand embroidery patterns bursting with spring flowers, we're delighted to be able to include the lovely Daisy the Felt Bird by Wendi Gratz, chat to some very talented makers and enjoy a piece of delicious lemon cake from Christina of Afrodite's Kitchen.

Next month is of course the month of love … and June's issue brings some beautiful dreamy makes - watch out for it on Thursday 28 May.

Happy stitching!

Helen xx

Tips for Stitchers

Fabrics that will be laundered should be washed before you begin stitching to ensure the fabric will not shrink afterwards. Carefully iron out any creases before you begin. This will make it easier to stitch evenly and will ensure you won't end up with wrinkles that you can't remove afterwards.

Between the Covers .....

Contributors

Rosie Studholme

Puts together all our lovely ideas, shopping and baking pages as well as researching & editing our features and interviews.

Hannah & Jessica

Have an amazing and eclectic stitching style and are the creative mother and daughter team behind Lady Jane Longstitches

Wendi Gratz

Of Shiny Happy World is on a mission to teach people that anyone can sew! Or quilt! Or embroider!

Alejandra of Epoque Graphics

Creates gorgeous prints, greetings cards and pocket mirrors which all feature her beautiful watercolour designs.

Shiran of Pretty Simple Sweet

Is a self-confessed dessert addict who constantly bakes and dreams of sweet things!

Annette of Oliver Rabbit

Has been stitching for over five decades and enjoy sharing her knowledge, inspiration and stories.

Lauren of Paper Doily Party Shop

Loves the pretty things in life - and used that love to start her own new business.

The merry month of May .....

May Day has been celebrated since ancient times, with various festivities. In the old Celtic calendar it is the first day of summer when cattle were led up into the hills to graze, marked by the festival of Beltane.

Better known today is the custom of going a-Maying which dates from the thirteenth century or even earlier in England. It is followed by the crowning of the May Queen - the prettiest girl in the village - and perhaps an ancient folk-memory of the Roman goddess Flora, who was worshipped in the five day festival of Floralia that took place round about this time in ancient Rome.

The focal point of British May Day festivities was, and still is, the Maypole - a tall pole decorated with flowers at its top and often painted with brightly coloured stripes. There are ribbons too, for each dance to grasp and create pretty coloured patterns by weaving in and out of each other as they dance around the pole.

A more restrained celebration still takes place in Oxford where people gather on Magdalen Bridge in the early hours of the morning to hear the choir of Magdalen College sing a Latin hymn at the top of the college tower at 6 am.

Today May 1st is also celebrated as Labour day by trades unions, socialists and workers movements. It is marked by rallies and marches, and sometimes by protests and riots, in countries across the world. Labour ay celebrations originated in the USA in 1867 when the working day was reduced from 10 to 8 hours, firstly in Illinois and later across the country.

One of the earliest surviving English folk customs is the Helston Furry Dance which takes place in the Cornish town of Helston on the eighth of May each year. Residents dance along the narrow streets of the town to a traditional tune played by the local band. Children dress in white, while the men wear top hats and morning coats with a lily-of-the-valley button hole and the women wear long dresses in bright summer colours and large fancy hats. The town is decorated for the occasion with flowers and greenery brought in from the countryside round about.

Just click on the image below to see a Pathe Newsreel of the Helston Furry Dance in 1951:

The Helston Furry dance was lovingly described in a song by the musician and composer Katie Moss written in 1911, and subsequently recorded by Terry Wogan in 1977.

A less famous, but immensely more important anniversary is May 14, the day that Edward Jenner inoculated a boy with matter from a pustule on the hand of a woman with cow pox. The boy was subsequently inoculated with small pox and discovered to be immune - the first signs of success in our battle against a deadly disease that was finally won in 2010 when smallpox was declared to have been eradicated worldwide.

This year sees the 70th anniversary of VE day on May 6, and also the 65th anniversary of Dunkirk when the "little ships" rescued more than 300,000 Allied troops from the beaches of Dunkirk during the Second World War.

And finally, if you're in England during May do be sure to make time to visit a bluebell wood. England is home to half the world's population of bluebells and the sight of a bluebell wood in full bloom simply takes your breath away!

7

Look!

a lovely idea

Watercolour Printable

Pretty up your home this Spring with a gorgeous watercolour printable from City Farm Girl. Best of all, you can download this wall art from Jen's website totally FREE!

LET NEW adventures BEGIN

FREE download: www.cityfarmhouse.com

BUSTLE & SEW
LOVE TO SEW AND SEW WITH LOVE

Workroom Embroidered Sign

I had such fun stitching this and it makes me smile every time I go past my workroom door. I just love the combination of pretty florals and flowing black text.

This sign isn't really too hard to stitch - I've used French knots, bullion stitch, back stitch, wheel stitch and straight stitch. The only slightly tricky stitch is bullion stitch, but it only takes a little practice to achieve good results.

I've included additional texts in case you'd like to hang your sign on a different door. My finished door sign is mounted in a 9" x 5" oval hoop.

Materials

- 12" x 8" cream fabric suitable for embroidery

- 9" x 5" oval hoop.

- DMC stranded cotton floss in shades 153, 310, 327, 519, 733, 818, 839, 904, 911 3078, 3350, 3708, 3862

Notes:

- Use two strands of floss throughout.

- The text is worked in 310 (black) floss

Notes on stitching

- Transfer your design to the centre of your cream fabric. The templates are given full size.

- Use two strands of floss throughout.

- The two colour flowers are worked in radiating straight stitch. I find it easiest to imagine a clock and place my first stitches at 3, 6, 9 and 12 o'clock then go around and fill in between them - this helps me make sure that they are even.

- The centres of the large flowers are French knots

- Bullion stitch is also used to make flowers - there are bullion stitch roses where the stitch is coiled around upon itself and also long flowers comprising three long bullion stitches.

To work bullion stitch bring your needle through your fabric at the point indicated by the arrow on the diagram above. Insert your needle back through your fabric at the required length of the stitch and bring it out exactly at the arrow again. Don't pull your needle right through, but leave it lying in the material as in the diagram and twist your thread around it close up to the emerging point.

Six or seven twists are an average number, but this can be varied according to the length of stitch you want to make. Place your left thumb upon the twists and pull your needle and thread through your fabric and also the twists as carefully as possible. Now pull your needle and thread away in the opposite direction. This movement will force your little coil of thread to lie flat in the right place. Tighten it up by pulling your working thread, then reinsert your needle at A.

733		153	
818		327	
3708		519	
3350		3078	
3862			
839			
503			
907			
904			
911			

The text is worked in satin and stem stitch. Angle your stitches to follow the curves of the letters and try to achieve a nice smooth flowing line. Alternative texts are included in the templates section at the back.

Bullion Stitch   French knots   Wheel stitch   French knots

Feather stitch   Radiating Straight Stitch   Back stitch

A (very) Little History of Knitting

Everyone is familiar with knitted items, and perhaps, inspired by sites such as Ravelry, may even have tried making their own scarves, jumpers or cushions. But did you know that knitting is actually an incredibly ancient craft, dating back possibly as far as 900 BC?

Academics have suggested that the fabled web (from Homer's Odyssey) worked by Penelope during the day and unpicked every night must have been knitted and not woven. If it had been woven, they believe, then far more time would have been require to unpick than to weave it; but if it were knitted then the work that had taken all day to complete could be undone in a matter of a few minutes without any difficulty at all. And if you require proof of this, then just ask any knitter who has ever experienced a parting of needle and stitches!!

Yarn, like most textiles, is of course extremely perishable so no actual knitted items still survive, and it isn't until much later - the mid-sixteenth century in fact, that we have enough evidence to follow its development fully.

The first knitting guild was set up in Paris in 1527, followed by others across Europe. Although today men don't often take up knitting, back then these guilds were male-dominated - women were spinners and the men were knitters and weavers. The only women admitted to the guilds were widows who, after their husbands' deaths, took on their work.

It was during Tudor times that knitting became popular both as a domestic craft and as a flourishing cottage industry, particularly in countries such as England where the wool trade made a major contribution to the economy. Indeed, knitting must have been a well-established craft in England by this time, for a law of 1565 stated that every person above the age of seven had to wear:

"Upon the Sabbath or holyday upon their head a cap of wool knitted, thickened and dressed in England."

Failure to wear a cap would result in your being fined for each day of transgression. Many of these Tudor caps can be seen in museums. They were hand knitted, then felted by immersion in water for a few days. Once the wool had thickened sufficiently the cap was blocked into shape, brushed with a teasel brush and could be cut without the knitting unravelling. The Turkish fez and French beret are still made in just the same way. Knitted stockings were also fashionable for the wealthy in England after Queen Elizabeth I was presented with a pair by a courtier.

But hand knitting went into a steep decline following the invention of the knitting machine by William Lee in 1589. His machine was able to produce knitted goods much faster than any hand knitter ever could. Knitting survived though as a domestic craft, as it does to this day.

In the nineteenth century knitters throughout Europe made garments for troops in various wars and some of these designs we still wear today. Did you know that the Battle of Balaclava in the Crimean war gave its name to the knitted helmets which covered the head, ears and necks of the soldiers who had to fight in the extreme cold?

It was around this time that the growth of the middle classes allowed women with time on their hands to take up various handicrafts, including lace knitting. Many fine lace stitches were invented at this time and used to make shawls, mittens, tablecloths and bonnets.

The advent of the circulating library and the introduction of ladies' journals and magazines helped to make knitting an even more popular craft, though in remote communities traditional patterns and designs continued to be handed down by word of mouth. It is claimed, for example, that today's traditional Fair Isle patterns are virtually unchanged from the original designs that are said to have been taught to the islanders by shipwrecked Spanish sailors after the attempted invasion of England by the Armada in the sixteenth century.

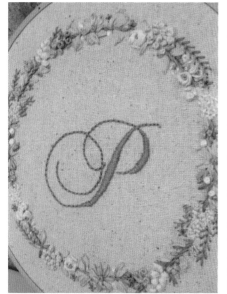

Meet the Maker

Jessica & Hannah **talk to us about their stitchy obsession, where they find their creative inspiration and how they started their business,** Lady Jane Longstitches

Lady Jane Longstitches is an Etsy shop run by mother-daughter hand embroidery artists and best friends Jessica Pambianco and Hannah Farabaugh in Willow Grove, Pennsylvania.

How did you get into embroidery?

Jessica: "My love for drawing and art began when I was a child, I would stand by my fathers side as he sat and created these amazing watercolor pieces, they are some of my earliest memories. I was in awe and knew I wanted to be an artist. I drew and also painted in watercolour, but I never went to school for art as I had hoped, I lacked confidence. One day in my 20's, when Hannah was quite young, I tried my hand at ribbon embroidery and loved it. This initial attempt at embroidery lasted a very short while because I was soon back in college earning my Nursing degree and then I had two more children. Life was hectic with 3 kids and I didn't start anything artistic again for over 12 years! Life was a tornado of dirt, tangled hair, appointments, wrangling, cooking, cleaning and exhaustion... I was feeling lost, like I needed a hobby to define myself as more than just a mother. I was searching on the internet and an embroidery pattern caught my eye, I ordered it and before I was halfway through stitching I was already drawing up my own patterns for hoops. It was an immediate fit for me. After I had been embroidering for about a year, Hannah was interested in learning, so I taught her the basics and she soon joined in with the same passion as me. Having my daughter as a partner was a natural fit, we may look nothing alike, but we think so much alike and are the best of friends and rarely argue. We help to motivate one another when we are bored of a project or just plain stuck and it's been a fantastic way to become closer than we already were. I couldn't be happier because I feel embroidery bonded us in a whole new way.

How did your business come about?

Hannah: We were so addicted to the relaxing nature of hand stitching that we just kept creating and creating and creating! Eventually we were running out of wall space! I was familiar with Etsy and showed my mom as she had never heard of it before. We did our research and discovered how easy it was to set up a shop, so we set a deadline and created a list of projects

and went at it, stitching for hours each day. It felt awesome to know that our hobby (obsession) could have more of a purpose and possibly bring in a little side money! We opened our Etsy shop in April of 2013 and have loved every minute since.

How did you choose your business name?

Jessica: When it came to choosing a name, it was hard, we went through quite a long list to begin with (Scarlett Thimblefingers, The Collywobblery, Wren House Stitchery, Threading Water,...my father helped come up with about 40 different names!) We both loved all things British, we voraciously read Jane Austen and Charles Dickens and wanted to incorporate this love into our shop name. We decided to take my grandmothers middle name, Jane, and turned it into a fun Austen/Dickens inspired combo, Lady Jane Longstitches was born! Since our style was so diverse, we used the tag line of "Properly Improper."

Do you have a favourite design you have made?

Jessica: Personally I am totally in love with my new landscape portraits. They feel free and relaxed, they are personal and real pieces of art versus "craft." I started creating these hoops from my own family vacation photos, as a way to capture our memories in a different media besides photography. It worked out so well on the 1st try that I made a 2nd, then a 3rd.....then I offered custom slots on our Instagram account as a way to build a portfolio and had an overwhelming response. I was blown away by the support from that community. I knew that this was my direction, I had found my voice, this was what I've been searching for!

Hannah: I love stitching artwork that involves flowers, leaves, or trees. I prefer anything that has to do with nature or gardening, it probably stems from my years working at a local florist and my desire to one day own my own homestead. I want herbs, fruit trees, vegetables and my own cottage garden full of all the flowers I can fit. I think this is reflected in my work. I adore the rainbow leaf garland hoop I made for my daughter Luna, it is happy and bright and I love seeing it hang on my wall. It makes me think of all the flowers I will one day grow

Why do you think there has been a resurgence in handmade?

Hannah: I think younger generations are looking for ways to be more self sufficient, the job market is tough to break into and making your own things, whether it's by homesteading or selling handmade goods is an ideal way to pave your own future. I think our generation is more heavily involved in wanting to know where their food and goods have come from, buying local and supporting artisans that are accessible to them brings them closer to the earth and to individual people and farther from mass produced consumerism. It's self empowering knowing that we can control our futures without having to leave our homes!

How does your creative process work?

Jessica: We gain inspiration from everything and anything it seems: a flower we saw on a walk, a quote we read in a Jane Austen book, a scene from a period movie, a song we got stuck in our head, a photograph we saw on the internet, or a trail we hiked while on vacation. We keep a sketch book of all our ideas and then pattern them out when the mood strikes, somewhat impulsively. I typically draw up the patterns and then we fight (nicely) over who can do what. We each have our own ideas of how we want to see things, but generally we

collaborate and seem to have the same aesthetic. Hannah loves to give me the finished pieces to hoop, she loves to rub it in saying, "Cutting and gluing are not my strong points since you never sent me to preschool." So I get stuck with the finish work, it's definitely not my favorite part of the process, I'd always rather be stitching!

What advice would you give anyone wanting to turn their hobby into a business?

Research and know your limits! If you have a skill or trade and you think you would like to make it more than a hobby, there is a ton of info at your fingertips to get started. Read articles from small business owners, hone your craft, be passionate about what you are creating, get to craft fairs and talk to people, be original, start small, but most of all be true to yourself. Realize that success doesn't happen over night. Our first year on Etsy we had maybe 20 sales, but we delighted in each one of those. We always felt surprised that someone out in the big world wanted our hoops and we nearly fell over when we had our first international sale! Once we built a base of sales and earned positive reviews from customers, our orders picked up. So despite how slowly the start is, there was a reward for not giving up! We are going to keep embroidering whether people buy our items or not, I think that passion shows.

Finally, could you please describe your style in a few words?

Eclectic! We started with embroidering snarky comments (and even some naughty curse words), song lyrics, and quotes and soon grew into nature themed items and our landscape portraits. We jokingly call ourselves the ADHD stitchery, we have had short attention spans and entertained this idea that we could stitch it all! Our idea book is filled with more concepts than we could ever possibly execute, hand embroidery is slow and patient work after all. Recently we have definitely narrowed our gaze, we have each found a direction that suits us more than the work we began with, the focus we now possess translates as pure confidence.

BUSTLE & SEW
LOVE TO SEW AND SEW WITH LOVE

Mini Hoop Pin Cushion

You can never have too many pin cushions - in my opinion at least - though I tend to use mine to stick various needles in as I'm stitching rather than to store pins.

This little pin cushion is super-easy to make - some simple embroidery that's easily within a the reach of a beginner mounted within a 3" hoop and filled with some toy stuffing. A nice firm cardboard base covered with a circle of felt finishes everything off nicely.

Materials

- 6" square white felt

- 3" hoop

- DMC stranded cotton floss in shades 703 (green), 827 (light blue), 3843 (bright blue) and 4120 (variegated

- Toy stuffing

- PVA glue (in which case you will need clips to hold the base in place while the glue dries) or a glue gun

- 4" square medium weight cardboard

- 4" square pale coloured felt for base

Notes:

- Use two strands of floss throughout.

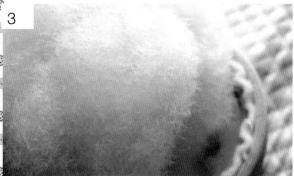

Method

- Transfer the pattern to the centre of your white felt and work the embroidery as follows:

- "Pins" chain stitch 3843

- Flowers radiating straight stitch 4120, centres French knots (or you could use small straight stitches if you're not confident with French knots) 827

- Leaves satin stitch worked at an angle to the centre of the leaves - pointing outwards and upwards 703

- When you've finished your embroidery press lightly on the reverse being careful not to flatten the stitches.

- Draw around the outer part of your hoop onto your card and pale felt. Cut out two circles, very slightly within the drawn line. Place to one side.

- Cut your felt into a 5" circle centred on your embroidery. Run a gathering stitch around the edge of the circle (1) and gather edges in to fit around the inner part of your hoop.

- Push the outer hoop down over the top and tighten screw slightly. Push your felt up into the hoop to form a dome shape. When you're happy with the shape tighten the screw fully and trim off any excess felt. (2)

- Push toy stuffing up into the dome shape and run a ring of glue around the bottom edge of the hoop. (3)

- Press card onto bottom of hoop. If you're using a glue gun hold until glue has set. If PVA then secure in place with clips until glue has dried (4)

- Glue circle of felt over cardboard base.

- Your pin cushion is now finished.

The Land in Spring ....

And for this summer's quick delight
Sow marigold, and sow the bright
Frail poppy that with noonday dies
But wakens to a fresh surprise;

Along the pathway stones be set
Sweet Alysson and mignonette,
That when the full midsummer's come
On scented clumps the bees may hum,
Golden Italians, and the wild
Black humble-bee alike beguiled:

And lovers who have never kissed
May sow the cloudy Love-in-Mist.

Extract from the poem by Vita Sackville-West

Perfect Lemon Cake

Ingredients

Cake:
> 1 1/2 cups (200 g/7 oz) all-purpose flour
> 1/2 teaspoon baking powder
> 1/4 teaspoon baking soda
> 1/4 teaspoon salt
> 1/2 cup buttermilk
> 1 tablespoon freshly squeezed lemon juice
> 1 1/2 tablespoons grated lemon zest (2 lemons)
> 3/4 cup plus 2 tablespoons (175 g/6.2 oz) granulated sugar
> 1/2 cup (1 stick/113g) butter, softened
> 2 large eggs, room temperature
> 1 teaspoon vanilla extract

Syrup:
> 1/4 cup granulated sugar
> 1/4 cup freshly squeezed lemon juice >
> (1-2 lemons)
> 2 teaspoons water

Glaze (optional):
> 1 tablespoon lemon juice
> 1 tablespoon milk
> 1 cup powdered sugar, sifted

Instructions

> In a medium bowl, sift together flour, baking powder, baking soda, and salt. In a small bowl, mix together buttermilk and lemon juice. Set bowls aside.

> In another small bowl, toss together sugar and lemon zest until combined. In a standing mixer fitted with the paddle attachment, beat together butter and sugar mixture on medium speed for 3 minutes until light and fluffy. Occasionally scrape down the sides and bottom of the bowl.

> Add eggs, one at a time, beating well after each addition. Beat in vanilla extract. On low speed, beat in the flour mixture in 3 parts, alternating with the buttermilk mixture in 2 parts, starting and ending with the flour. Do not over mix.

> Scrape batter into prepared pan and smooth the top. Bake for 40-60 minutes or until a skewer inserted into the centre of the cake comes out clean. If the top is browning too fast while baking, cover pan loosely with aluminium foil.

> For the syrup: While cake is in the oven, prepare the syrup. In a small saucepan, combine sugar, lemon juice, and water. Cook on medium-low heat until sugar dissolves and syrup forms. Set aside to cool.

> When the cake is done, allow to cool for 10 minutes, then remove from pan and set on a wire rack. Place a

tray or pan underneath the wire rack. Poke cake with a toothpick, then brush top and sides with syrup. Allow cake to cool to room temperature.

> For the glaze: In a small bowl, combine sugar, lemon juice, and milk, and whisk until smooth. Add more lemon juice or sugar as necessary until you get a thick yet pourable consistency. Pour over top of cake and let drizzle down the sides. Allow glaze to set, 15-30 minutes.

> Store cake in an airtight container at room temperature for up to 3-4 days or in the refrigerator for up to 5 days. Cake can be frozen without the syrup or glaze for up to 2 months. Once thawed, heat the syrup and drizzle hot over the cake, then proceed with the rest of the recipe and make the glaze.

We chat to Shiran from Pretty Simple Sweet, a self confessed dessert addict who constantly bakes and dreams of sweet things...

When did you first start making & baking cakes?

While I've always loved desserts, I only started baking a few years ago. It was only when I moved out to my own apartment that I actually had to start making my own food, and food to me means *desserts.*

Do you have a favourite baker who inspires you?

I draw inspiration from so many bakers and cookbook authors! Alice Medrich, Dorie Greenspan, Rose Levy Be-ranbaum, and Pierre Herme are some of my favourites, to name a few.

Any tips for someone wanting to start a baking blog?

Be persistent. It takes time to grow a blog, but if it's truly your passion and you put your heart and soul into it, it will eventually come together. Also, while getting inspiration from other bloggers that you love is important, remember that what might work for others may not work for you. Stay true to yourself and don't lose sight of what you really love. My last bit of advice would be to not try to be perfect all the time – just have fun with it.

Be sure to pop over to Shiran's lovely blog, www.prettysimplesweet.com, for lots more delicious recipes!

Gisela Graham Spotted Pastel Mini Heart
Dishes, Mollie & Fred
www.molliandfred.co.uk

Pink Heart Doilies, Hampton Blue
www.hamptonblue.co.uk

Star Baker

Bake in style with
these gorgeous
goodies!

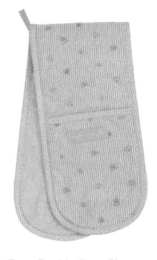

Apron, Ville & Campagne
www.villeetcampagne.co.uk

Rose Double Oven Gloves,
Sophie Allport
www.sophieallport.com

Pink Baking Cups Set,
Candle & Cake Ltd
www.candleandcake.co.uk

Painted Geometric Utensil Set,
Etsy
www.hollyhorton.etsy.com

Wooden Cake Topper,
Ginger Ray
www.gingerray.co.uk

BUSTLE & SEW

LOVE TO SEW AND SEW WITH LOVE

Mr Toad Softie

Mr Toad is the second in my series of Wind in the Willows-inspired softies.

He's stitched from felt, and there is just a little machine stitching to form his neck and belly, but you could always use a short stab stitch if you would prefer to sew him completely by hand. His mouth is a line of chain stitch and he has two black beady eyes.

Toad measures around 5" tall when sitting.

Materials

- 8" square of dark and light green felt

- 2" square or less of gold felt

- Black and green embroidery floss or cotton pearl thread

- Toy stuffing

- Two ¼" black beads

Notes:

- Apart from the dart and centre seam at the front all the pieces are joined by hand using two strands of floss and cross stitch. This gives a nice strong decorative finish. To do this place the pieces to be joined with wrong sides together. Stitch half cross stitch in one direction, then return the opposite way to complete the stitch.

Method

- Cut out all pieces in accordance with the templates

- Join the two front pieces from A to B and from A to C by machine with the WRONG sides together. Use a 1/8" seam allowance. You join them like this as you don't want a ridge running right down the middle of his chin and belly.

- Now stitch the dart from A to A in the same way. This forms his chin.

- With RIGHT sides facing and using cross stitch join the back and front pieces together round from D to D.

- Stuff the body before the gap gets too small. Make the stuffing quite firm, but not too much so as you don't want to put excessive strain on the under-chin dart.

- Join arm and leg pieces. Each limb comprises one light green and one dark green piece. Begin joining them from the middle of the bottom edge, and stuff as you go - the limbs are quite thin and will be hard to stuff if you wait until you're nearly done.

- You will find a stuffing stick is really useful for pushing little pieces of stuffing into the ends of the limbs. Just break the pointed end off a bamboo skewer and fray the end so it "grabs" the stuffing as you push.

- Stitch arms and legs to the sides of the bodies. Note the upwards direction marked on the template - Mr Toad's limbs have a definite "up" and "down" side.

- Still using cross stitch, attach the eyelids to the eyes, joining the STRAIGHT edge of the green eyelid to the CURVED edge of the yellow eye (it feels wrong I know, but trust me!)

- Stitch the curved edge of the eye into place on the top of the head. Stuff lightly (you will really need your stuffing stick here), then stitch down the front of the yellow eye piece using short straight stitches.

- Stitch black beads into place for eyeballs, pulling slightly so that they sit firmly against the yellow eyes.

- Work a line of chain stitch around the curved edge of the head to represent the mouth.

- Your toad is now finished.

Choosing Your Thread

Whether by machine or by hand, we can't sew without thread! How many times, though, have you found yourself at the checkout counter of your favourite fabric store, uttering, "Oh, yes, I need thread!?" And you simply grab a spool from the nearest rack, in a matching colour of course, but without much thought as to what type or brand might produce the best results for your project. I know I'm guilty.

Does it really matter which thread you use? Yes, it does. Thread comes in a wide variety of fibres, sizes and quality levels. In order for your thread to produce strong and durable seams without being obtrusive on your fabric, you need to choose it wisely.

COMMON TYPES OF SEWING THREADS

Cotton Thread

Cotton thread (in a medium thickness, size 50) is best suited for projects using lightweight to medium-weight, natural woven fabrics such as cotton, linen and rayon. Most cotton thread is mercerized - a finishing process that leaves the thread smooth and lustrous. Cotton thread is softer than polyester. It also has very little "give" (elasticity) and will ensure your project, such as a pieced quilt, holds it shape. This said, it is not a good choice for stretchy fabrics!

Cotton thread is a favourite among quilters who are sewing with high-quality quilting fabric. The 50-weigh in a neutral colour is ideal for piecing, appliqué and binding, whereas a heavier 28-weight is best for quilting. It must withstand the stress of pulling and stretching. Quilting cotton is available coated, allowing the thread to pass through quilt fabric and batting with ease, or you can wax your thread as you go. Only use coated quilting cotton for hand quilting, as the coating will gum up your sewing machine.

Polyester Thread

Polyester thread is truly an all-purpose thread and is suitable for most sewing projects. It is a good choice for woven synthetics, knits and fabrics with stretch in them because it has some "give" to it and won't break easily. Most polyester threads are treated with a wax or silicone coating, which enables the thread to slide through fabric easily. Polyester thread is widely available and offered in a vast spectrum of colors, making fabric coordination a breeze.

Cotton Covered Polyester Thread

Cotton covered polyester is an all-purpose thread combining the strength and elasticity of a polyester core with an exterior wrapping of cotton filament for durability and heat resistance. If your fabric requires high heat for pressing, this is a good thread variety to use. Blended threads are well suited for nearly all fabrics, including natural or synthetic, wovens or knits.

Silk Thread

Pure silk thread is made from natural fibres and is recognized for its beauty and durability. It is very fine and comes in a variety of weights and colours. Silk thread has elasticity and is well suited for thin delicate fabrics such as those used in lingerie. Use it when sewing with silk fabrics and wool. It is also an excellent choice for basting, as it won't leave imprint "holes" in your fabric once it is removed. Silk thread is a popular choice for hand and machine appliqué projects because the thread "melts" into your fabric, making your stitches nearly invisible. **Do not confuse pure silk thread with "silk finish" cotton thread, a soft and lustrous top quality sewing thread made of double-mercerized 100% cotton. This thread has low shrinkage, provides seam elasticity, is exceptionally colourfast and safe to iron.

SPECIALTY THREADS

Heavy-duty Thread

Heavy-duty threads are more coarse, usually a size 40 or thicker, and stronger than all-purpose threads. They can be cotton, polyester and cotton/poly blends. Not suited for most garment construction, this type of thread is a great choice when using upholstery-weight fabrics for home decorating projects such as couch cushions or window shades. It is also a great choice for heavy denim projects and items such as backpacks where a finer thread will break.

Button and Craft Thread

Button and craft thread is exceptionally strong and thicker than all-purpose threads. It is most commonly used to sew on buttons by hand. It is also used for top stitching and soft sculpture sewing when a strong thread is needed. Don't be tempted to use it for regular sewing projects, even when you think a stronger thread is needed. A thread too thick for your project will appear obtrusive.

Invisible Thread

Invisible thread is intended for just that purpose - to be invisible! No longer compared to "fishing line," today's invisible thread is soft and light. It is available in polyester or nylon and comes in different colorations and sheen levels. It is commonly used for sewing garment labels, multi-coloured bindings, tapes and patches. Also a favourite for machine quilting, it allows the sewer to span multi-coloured piecework without changing colours.

Nylon Thread

Nylon thread is a synthetic fibre appreciated for its strength and flexibility. This thread is lightweight, smooth and suitable for light to medium weight synthetic fabrics such as nylon tricot, suede cloth, faux fur and fleece. A nylon seam will "last forever."

Why is the quality of your thread important?

I love a bargain. Who doesn't? But when it comes to sewing, I want a quality finished product and the best way to achieve that is to use quality components. Your sewing machine would agree with me.

Among other characteristics, better quality threads are made of long, tightly woven fibres while economical ones have short, loose, stray fibres - fibres that can get stuck in your fabric and in your sewing machine while you sew. You can't see these loose fibres with the naked eye but I can assure you they are there. These little "strays," we'll call them, rub against the thread, leaving it weak and subject to breakage, both while you're sewing and later in the seam itself. These little fibres also clog your sewing machine's tension disks - the little devices that control the pressure as your upper thread travels through your machine - and affect your machine's ability to maintain an evenly formed stitch.

Oliver Rabbit

Hello! I'm Annette and Oliver Rabbit is my labor of love. I've been stitching for over five decades and enjoy sharing my knowledge, inspiration and stories, both past and present, about the magic of making something.

www.oliverrabbit.com

Daisy the felt bird

You will need
> less than 1 sheet of purple sage felt for the body

> scraps of strawberry dream and straw felt for the comb and beak

> one sheet Sulky Sticky FabriSolvy (optional, but strongly recommended)

> embroidery thread

> polyfill stuffing

> needle

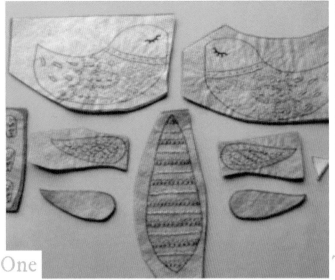

One

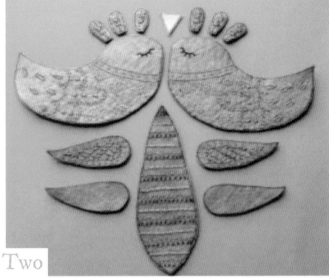

Two

Three

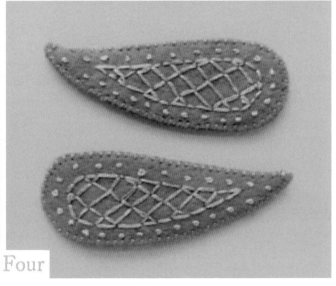

Four

Step one:

Print the pattern onto a sheet of Sulky Sticky Fabri-Solvy. Stick it to the felt and stitch right through it. Everything is stitched with two strands of floss in the following stitches: Eye - backstitch, Neck band - split stitch and Frenchknots, Starbursts - backstitch, Aster-isks - backstitch, Drops at tail - lazy daisy, Wide belly stripes - backstitch, Narrow belly stripes - chain stitch, Wings - backstitch and French knots, Comb - lazy daisy the flower and the leaves. Backstitch the stem.

If you choose not to use the Sulky Sticky FabriSolvy you can use your favorite method of transferring the design to felt, but this stuff makes it really easy!

Step two:

Cut out each piece carefully on the lines. Be sure not to cut into any of your stitching. Soak them in cool water to remove the stabilizer and let them dry flat on a towel. Don't wring them out just lay them on a towel dripping wet and they'll dry overnight. From here on all the sewing is whipstitch around the edges of the felt. I used two strands of floss for all whipstitching.

Step three:

Put comb pieces together, right sides facing out, and stitch all the way around the edge. You'll end up with three comb pieces.

Step four:

Repeat Step 3 for the wings, pairing one embroidered wing with one blank wing. The blank sides of the wings will go up against the bird's body where you can't see them.

Five

Six

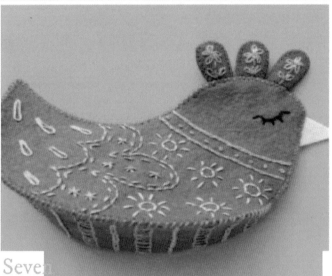

Seven

Eight

Step five:

Place the two body pieces right sides facing out, with the comb pieces sandwiched between the layers. Stitch the body pieces together along the top edge of the body. Stop when you get to the tip of the tail, but don't tie off your thread.

Step six:

When you get to the tip of the tail, slip the belly piece into place. The narrow end is the tail, and the wider end is the breast. Stitch one body piece to one side of the belly piece. When you get to the front, stop stitching, but don't tie off your thread,

Step seven:

Go back to stitching the two body pieces together, this time stitching up the front of the face. Slip the beak in between the two layers, right up at the top of the face, and stitch through it as you go. Tie off your thread when you get to the top of the face.

Step eight:

Flip the bird over. Start a new piece of thread and stitch the free side of the body to the free side of the belly, starting at the front tip of the belly. Stitch for a few inches, then tie off your thread.

Nine

Ten

Step nine:

With a new piece of thread stitch the rest of the body closed from the tail to the other side of the stuffing opening you started in Step 8. Stuff the body neatly. You can add plastic pellets if you like, for weight, but this shape doesn't need it for balance.

Step ten:

Sew up the rest of the stuffing opening. Now she's just waiting for wings! Thread a long needle and knot the end. Start sewing underneath one wing, near the front. Sew through the body and out the other side, through the opposing wing. Take a small stitch back into the wing, through the body and out through the first wing. Stitch back and forth like this a few times to secure the wings. Don't pull the thread too tight or you'll distort the shape of her body. Knot your thread underneath one wing and bury the tail.

You can find video tutorials for all stitches used in this pattern on Wendi's website, please click HERE.

shiny happy world

Before starting Shiny Happy World, Wendi Gratz spent over twenty years working in the children's book indstry. Now she lives in the mountains of North Carolina where she spends her time designing sewing, quilting and embroidery patterns especially for beginners.

Wendi says, "I'm on a mission to teach people that anyone can sew! Or quilt! Or embroider! All my patterns are designed especially for beginners and I never release a pattern until I have videos teaching every single skill needed for the project. It's the whole foundation of what I do and it's all because of my experience as a learner and as a teacher. I'm a self-taught sewist, and I learned before there was an internet. I still have such vivid memories of struggling with the instructions in patterns and sewing books!"

www.shinyhappyworld.com

BUSTLE & SEW
LOVE TO SEW AND SEW WITH LOVE

Gardener's Apron

I'm a bit of a fair-weather gardener I have to confess, but by May I'm usually to be found outdoors fairly regularly digging , weeding and pruning. And now I have this apron, I may be tempted outside a little earlier this year!

This is a really easy make, with some simple raw-edge applique, and would be a great project for a beginner. You could customise your apron with more loops for shears etc if you wanted, and there are two nice long tapes to wrap around your body.

Finished dimensions 23" wide and 16" long, though it's easy to adjust the length if you wish.

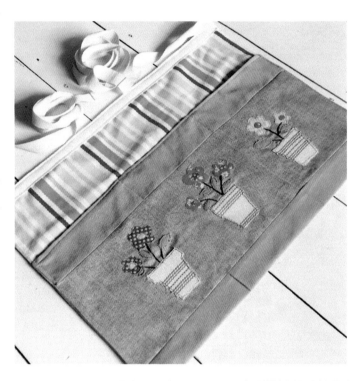

Materials

- 24" x 30" medium weight patterned cotton fabric (the striped fabric in my picture).

- 24" x 23" medium weight plain cotton fabric (green)

- 24" x 9" neutral cotton fabric

- Scraps of cotton fabric for applique work

- 3 yards x 1" cream cotton twill tape

- Dark green embroidery floss

- Bondaweb

- Temporary fabric marker pen

- Grey or green and cream sewing thread

- Embroidery foot for your machine.

Note: use ½" seam allowance

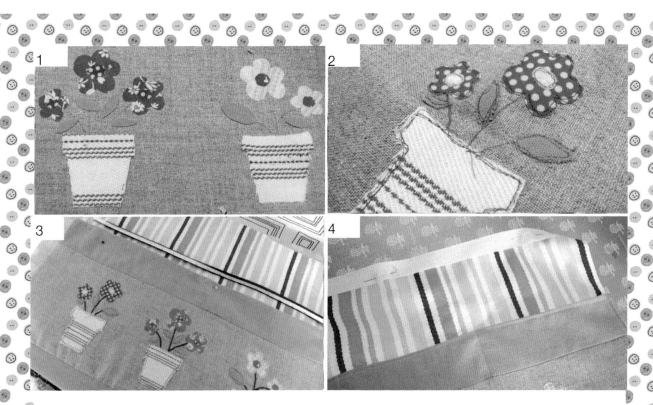

Method

- Cut 3" strip from one end of your plain fabric and place to one side

- Create your plant pot applique. Trace the applique shapes onto the paper side of your Bondaweb. The plant pot is the same for each flower so is only given once - trace it three times. Note the plant with three flowers is in the centre.

- Fold your strip of neutral coloured fabric into three and press the folds with your hands. This will help you position your plants. Place the two outer plants slightly towards the centre of the rectangle you formed with your creases so they don't disappear round to the sides of the apron when it is being worn.

- First position the plant pots - the bases are 1 ½" up from the bottom of your fabric. Fuse into place then draw in the stems of the plants with your temporary fabric marker pen using the template as a guide.

- Now cut and fuse the flowers and the flower centres in the same way. (1)

- Fit the embroidery foot to your sewing machine and drop the feed dogs.

- With grey or green thread in your needle and cream in your bobbin stitch around the edges of your applique shapes. Go around twice for a sort of scribbled effect. There is no need to lift your needle between shapes, just stitch up the temporary fabric marker lines you drew. (2)

- With three strands of dark green floss work the stems in chain stitch along the lines you drew. This will cover the stitching between shapes. Press your work lightly on the reverse.

- Join the bottom of the applique panel to one end of your plain fabric, and then attach the 3" strip along the top.

- Place your patterned fabric and your plain fabric/applique panel right sides together and machine stitch around the edges leaving a 6" gap at the top for turning.

- Clip corners and turn right side out. Press well, rolling the seams between your fingers and thumb to make sure they're completely open. Press edges of turning gap to inside and press well.

- Place your panel with the patterned side upwards on a clean flat surface. Now fold up the bottom edge - revealing the applique design - by 11" to form the deep pocket and pin (3)

- Topstitch all the way round your apron 1/4" from the edge. Go backwards and forwards over the pocket top for extra strength. Press again.

- To divide the pocket sew vertically from the bottom to the top of the pocket forming three equally sized pockets. Work from the bottom to the top so that if your fabric stretches slightly the bottom of the apron won't become twisted and distorted. Again go backwards and forwards over the top of the pocket for extra strength

- For the tie, pin and then sew the length of twill tape along the top of the apron (4). There should be plenty to allow the tie to warp around and then be tied at the front.

- Turn over and hem the raw ends of the tape to prevent fraying.

- Your apron is now finished.

The Cutting Garden

One of the nicest things we did for Rosie and Dan's wedding last year was to establish a Cutting Garden in a sheltered spot beside the old stone wall. We had so many flowers, not only to decorate the barn where the reception was held, but to enjoy all summer long as our garden just kept flowering. Our plot measured only around 10 x 12 foot, but we had plenty of blooms and enough to keep friends and neighbours supplied too. If you've been thinking about a cutting garden of your own then now is the time to start putting your plans into action.

Establishing a cutting garden means that you don't need to rob your borders of their best blooms to bring flowers into the house - and even if you don't have a lot of space, a row of flowers squeezed in between the cabbages and beans of your vegetable patch will produce more than enough flowers to keep a vase on your table all summer through.

Once you've decided where your cutting garden will be you will need to clear the ground of weeds. But don't fertilize or manure it heavily, as rich soil may often produce lush, soft green growth at the expense of flowers. It's a bit late for spring this year, but when planting bulbs in the autumn cram as many daffodils and tulips as you can into your allotted space. You can safely ignore the recommended spacing distances for these bulbs as you are not making a permanent planting. As you are likely to be picking these flowers when the ground is wet and muddy it's worth planting them in blocks or rows with planks between to use as paths so you can reach them easily when you want to cut them.

In our garden we planted some plug plants, but also raised a lot from seed - cottage garden annuals are particularly easy for this and they make particularly charming summer posies. Try cosmos (we were particularly successful with these, godetia, love-in-a-mist, larkspur and sweet scabious. Plant your seeds in straight rows so it's easy to tell the difference between flowers and weeds when they start to germinate. You will probably need to thin them as they grown - be sure to refer to the seed packet for further instructions.

I hate pulling out perfectly healthy baby plantlets, but if you don't do this then they will all be fighting for space and nutrients and the results will be disppointing.

For tall arrangements grow hollyhocks, verbena, delphiniums and honesty. Plant your delphiniums, together with any other perennial flowers you choose, such as foxgloves, phlox or verbascum in a corner of your plot so there's no need to disturb them when you clear your plot at summer's end.

Always cut your flowers in the early morning when their moisture and sugar content is high. Take a bucket of water with you into the garden and plunge their stems into the water as soon as they are cut. When you are ready to arrange your flowers, re-cut them underwater to avoid getting an airlock in the stems that would slow down their uptake of water.

The milky sap of poppies and dahlias can contaminate the water in a vase of flowers and prevent the other species from taking up water. To stop the sap from leaking out seal the ends of poppies and dahlias by holding them in the flame of a match or candle for a few seconds.

If you do have a problem with slugs and don't want to use chemicals, then try turning their habit of hiding in the day against them. Setting out grapefruit halves or pieces of wood/bricks or stone and then turning them over usually reveals quite a few slugs - ugh!

Creating barriers is another way of deterring slugs without resorting to chemicals. Rings of soot, crushed eggshells, pine needles, ash and slaked lime sprinkled around vulnerable plants can work - although in my experience with varying degrees of success.

A more successful - though perhaps not very attractive trick is to cut the bottom off a clear plastic drinks bottle and use this as a mini-cloche to protect a small plant. Be sure to inspect the soil around the plant before you do this - there's nothing more annoying than trapping a slug alongside your precious baby plant!

"Start where you are with the tools you have"

Epoque Graphics

Alejandra talks to us about drawing and painting, her love of period dramas and how she started her business, Epoque Graphics

Alejandra runs her business from a home studio in London. She creates gorgeous prints, greetings cards and pocket mirrors which all feature her beautiful watercolour designs.

When did you start drawing and painting?

I have always loved drawing and painting. I guess I started when I was able to grab a pencil. I remember my mum teaching me how to paint simple things: a house, the sun, a person, a tree, a dog. She painted beautifully (and still does) and that always amazed me. I wanted to draw as beautifully as she did. When I was a child I could spend hours drawing. I had a big pouch full with crayons and it was one of my treatures. Matching my colours were so important for me (and still are). I remember looking around and checking the colours and shapes of things and the things that were around me before I started drawing. I liked to paint in detail and I really enjoyed that. I was lucky enough to attend a school where creativity was valued and encouraged and drawing was one of the activities we did to express ourselves.

How did your business come about?

I always wanted to have my own business, it was my dream. My dad had his own business, so I knew it was possible for me. Though I loved painting and creating in general when I was little, life took a very different path. Recently I took up painting again, first as a hobby and then I realised, living in an inspiring city such as London, and finding so many talented people online, that I could do the same, that I should give it a try. I started first printing greeting cards with my art, then stationery and prints, followed by other gifts. And the reception has been amazing! I am so happy with how my business has grown.

What advice would you give anyone who wants to turn their hobby into a business?

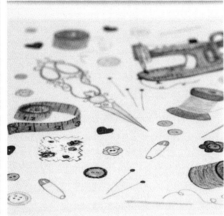

I remember reading a wonderful piece of advice on Pinterest: "start where you are with the tools that you have ". For me they were like magic words. I became aware that you don't need to wait for the perfect moment and have every detail perfect to do what you want. It's an organic process. Maybe you have a couple of tools (in my case some watercolours, brushes and paper), enough to get started. I am a great believer in learning by doing. You just need to dare to try things. At the same time, having your feet on the ground is important because you will need to know what works and what doesn't.

It's hard work in the beginning and you will need to persevere. You need to put your heart and soul into it, know that things won't happen alone and that it takes time. It is important to be super organised with the numbers, the deliveries, the packaging, taxes, etc. I would add that from the beginning it is very useful to use social media channels to promote your work. To provide excellent customer service is crucial too and finally, remember to have fun!

What projects are you working on at the moment?

I am a big fan of quotes, literature and wise words, so I am working on different paintings featuring words of encouragement and happiness, similar to the one I did with the lovely quote by the famous writer Louisa May Alcott.

I am planning to design more notebooks and matching pocket mirrors and to paint more greeting cards to expand the collection. I am also thinking about creating a special illustrated piece that those who enjoy cooking and baking will like very much. And if I have the chance I would love to paint a calendar! I really have so many ideas.

How does your creative process work?

I normally like to use any quiet moments I have, for example, before going to sleep, when my home is silent, to imagine things.

I create images in my mind very clearly with my eyes closed. It is like designing, sketching and painting in my head. I then make more detailed notes in my tablet. When I read the notes later, I remember the images I created in my head. Then, when I have the time, I start sketching the ideas for the illustrations and paintings I want to create. When I am happy with the results I start painting them (my favorite part). I then use my computer to add the finishing touches!

Where do you look for creative inspiration?

My eyes are always wide open to finding ideas and inspiration everywhere I go: it can be a café, a bookshop, a museum or simply walking through the streets. A movie can be a source of inspiration too, the era in which is set, for example. And Pinterest is a great place to find inspiration! I like to collect tons of images in my account and look at them to turn on my creativity. And of course, I find inspiration looking at the work that other creatives and artists create. It is great for checking up what is trending too!

Do you have a dedicated work room?

I have a little space in my home which I like to call my studio. There, I have all the tools of the trade and some books. I like to keep everything organised and at hand, so I don't waste time looking for things. There I draw, paint, edit, print, sort, pack and photograph products. I keep a mood board too, in which I pin some inspirational images, some of my works, a calendar and notes.

Finally, can you tell us about your typical day?

I normally wake up early in the mornings. I have a beautiful alarm clock, my lovely six month old baby (luckily I'm a morning person anyway!). I stay in bed for a bit, checking Instagram, Twitter and some of my favourite blogs. I love to break my goals for the day into small steps, so I write down on my notepad what I want to accomplish that particular day. Then I try to fit them around my baby's needs. In general, I spend some days drawing, others painting and a few more doing some paperwork. I take a couple of hours to cook something healthy for lunch. Normally I go to the post office during the afternoons, sending the items that my beloved customers have bought and at the end of the day, I like to have a light dinner with my husband, go to bed early and snuggle down under my duvet. I then like to read a good book or watch a period drama such as "Mr. Selfriges", "Downton Abbey", "Call the Midwife", "Grand Hotel" or "Velvet". But of course, neither of them can compare with my always beloved "Pride and Prejudice BBC TV series" from 1995!

Epoque Graphics

Alejandra has very kindly given all Bustle & Sew readers 15% off everything in her shop! Just enter the code 'SEWLOVE' at checkout.

www.epoquegraphics.com
@EPOQUEGRAPHICS

BUSTLE & SEW

LOVE TO SEW AND SEW WITH LOVE

Comfortable Cushion

I love the current trend for combining colourful florals with distinctive text. It's most usually seen in hand embroidery, but I thought it would be fun to try a different approach by scaling up my design and combining it with some freestyle machine applique using cheerful coloured felt, and just a little simple hand stitching.

British readers of a certain age will recognise the text from "Listen with Mother!" It's embroidered in split stitch whilst the floral garland uses chain stitch and French knots.

Cover fits 16" square pad

Materials

- ½ yard taupe gingham medium weight cotton fabric (mine was from Clarke and Clarke)

- Whole skein black stranded embroidery floss, as well as dark purple, red, light green and dark brown

- Felt in assorted greens and colours of your choice for flowers and berries. I used a light, medium and dark green, then terracotta, gold, pale yellow, cerise, pale pink and turquoise colours

- Bondaweb/temporary fabric adhesive spray

- Embroidery foot for your sewing machine.

- Cream and dusty green sewing thread

- Temporary fabric marker pen

Method

- From your gingham fabric cut one 16" square and two 12" x 16" rectangles. Put the rectangles to one side for the moment. (I always make my covers the exact size of the pad - they are a little snug to begin with, but as the cushion is used and the filling compacts, they end up fitting perfectly and the cushion holds its shape much better too).

- Transfer the text to this square, positioning it centrally vertically and with the top of the "A" 3" down from the top edge.

- Work the text. Outline in back stitch then fill with split stitch using 3 strands of floss. Black floss is very forgiving as you can't see the individual stitches very well, however do try to follow the shapes and curves of the letters with your stitching.

- Press your work lightly on the reverse.

- Using the reversed template, trace the flower and larger leaf shapes onto the paper side of your Bondaweb. You can also do this with the smaller leaf shapes, however I simply cut pointy ovals freehand and used spray adhesive to keep them in place while stitching - I found Bondaweb a bit fiddly for this - it's just a matter of choice though.

- Using the template as a guide position the shapes for the flower and leaf cluster, positioning the top flower approx 1 ½" below the "o" in comfortable. (1) Work from the bottom upwards - so start with the turquoise leaves, then the yellow flower, oak leaf, pink flower and finally the reddish brown flower. Don't fuse the shapes into place until you're totally happy with their positioning. Be sure to protect the felt from your hot iron with a cloth when fusin.

- Draw in the lines for your stems with your temporary fabric marker pen. They are just simple curves. Then position your leaves and pink berries along the lines. Just randomly mix the greens for the leaves. Again fuse into place.

- Fit the embroidery foot to your sewing machine and drop the feed dogs.

- With dusty green thread in your needle and a paler colour in your bobbin machine stitch around the edges of the felt shapes. Go around twice - don't be too neat, you're aiming for a sort of scribbled effect. If you're confident work the veins on the leaves (3) by machine too.

- Now embroider the hand stitched details (4)

- Add details using all six strands of floss as follows:

  ❑ Reddish brown flower has closely worked radiating long straight stitches in red floss, with a cluster of French knots in dark purple at the centre.

  ❑ Pink flower has two long straight stitches in red floss down the centre of each petal.

  ❑ Yellow flower has a cluster of purple French knots at the centre

- Add details using three strands of floss as follows:

  ❑ Pale pink berries have three or four straight stitches in dark brown floss at the top ends. Then a few purple stitches.

  ❑ Stems are worked in chain stitch using dark brown floss.

  ❑ Veins on oak leaf are long straight stitches in green floss.

- When your embroidery is finished press lightly on the reverse. Now make up the cushion cover.

- Turn over and hem one long edge on each of your rectangular pieces. This will form the two back parts of a simple envelope closure.

- Place your front panel right side up on a clean flat surface. Place the two back panels on top, right sides down aligning side edges so they overlap at the centre. Pin or baste.

- Machine around the edge of your cushion using a ½" seam allowance. (I usually go around twice for added strength and durability). Zig-zag, serge or cut raw edges with pinking shears.

- Turn right side out. Insert cushion pad and relax!

Discovering Sashiko

We are all familiar with the idea of the white cherry blossom seen against a blue sky as Japan celebrates Cherry Blossom season through April and May. But are you familiar with the blue and white of traditional Sashiko stitching?

Sashiko is the traditional form of stitching from northern Japan and uses running stitch to create intricate designs – usually worked in white or cream thread on an indigo blue background.

Patterns were handed down by the women of the families in these fishing and farming communities – their sashiko designs created a unique and individual style. Sashiko was an artisan craft – invented to quilt together layers of fabric for warm clothing, recycling old and damaged textiles as part of the quilting, and also lending strength to working garments which were often subject to a great deal of wear and tear.

Sashiko developed over the two centuries between the early 17th and mid-19th centuries probably beginning as someone repaired damaged clothes economically by using undyed thread on dark blue indigo cloth – then realising the decorative potential in the stitches they were making. At this time all fibres would have been

hand spun, woven and dyed from natural fibres including linen and hemp. The thrifty communities would have continually recycled – cloth may have begun life as a garment, then been re-purposed into bags and aprons, finally ending its life as a cleaning rag – every thread created during what would have been a very labour-intensive process was far too precious to throw away.

By the early 20th century Sashiko was accepted as a winter occupation when the usual heavy snowfall in the north of Japan meant that work outside was very limited. Sashiko skills were vital for young women and girls to acquire if they wanted to make a good marriage – learning Sashiko helped to develop patience and perseverance – essential for a farmer's wife.

Vintage Sashiko consists of two or three layers of fabric, with the best on top, and even the most complicated designs are achieved with simple running stitch.

Modern Sashiko may have only one layer of fabric or use polyester or cotton quilt wadding. As part of the recycling process vintage Sashiko uses layers of old or worn fabric instead of wadding, so it's much flatter than our western quilts. The stitches create a textured, flowing design sitting as they do on the fabric surface.

The traditional indigo and white colours used give Sashiko work dramatic visual impact, though over time the creamy cotton thread often took on a pale ice blue tint due to the migration of the dye. These colours were used in response to Edo sumptuary laws which prevented the lower classes from wearing brightly coloured and patterned clothing. Ordinary people could use indigo, with patterns no larger than a grain of rice or with stripes no wider than the width of a straw. This may be the origin of the idea that Sashiko stitches must resemble grains of rice. It is also said to represent snow lying on the ground.

By the mid-20th century however, increased prosperity, commercialisation and the introduction of man made fibres meant that, like other artisan cultures across the world, the way country folk dressed began to change and the art of Sashiko declined. Many garments were discarded, or destroyed in other ways. In the 1970s though, as western-style quilting became more popular in Japan, the art of Sashiko stitching was rediscovered. Modern stitchers appreciate working in the Sashiko style for its creative and relaxing qualities.

Modern Sashiko from Sake Puppets (CC Flickr)

Kendo Undergarment 19th Century
Kendo is a form of martial arts using bamboo rods practised by the Samurai.

BUSTLE & SEW
DIY Embroidery Stitch Video Shorts

Check out our library of FREE "how to" embroidery stitch videos

http://bustleandsew.com/free-patterns-download/diy-embroidery-tutorials/

rn Sashiko from ... rts (CC Flickr)

PAPER DOILY

Party Shop

We spoke to Lauren **about turning her dream into a reality, her hopes for the future and the inspiration behind** Paper Doily Party Shop

When you get married people often talk about enjoying your new life together – but Lauren's wedding wasn't only the beginning of married life, it also sowed the seeds of her successful online business, Paper Doily Party Shop. Whilst she was planning her wedding last year, Lauren discovered she absolutely loved researching, sourcing and buying party products. Indeed she was so good at it, that several of her guests made comments on her decorations, describing her reception as "magical." It was then that she realised she'd found something incredibly enjoyable and that she never wanted the party to end. Since her wedding, and following some careful planning, Paper Doily Party Shop was born when Lauren left her permanent job to focus on her business full-time.

Lauren originally trained at the Chelsea College of Art and Design, graduating with a degree in Textile Design. Her main specialisms were Printed Textiles and Embroidery and, after graduating, she worked in London for several companies, including Laura Ashley, The White Company and LK Bennett before moving to Bath where she worked for the local university.

Life these days though no longer involves a daily commute to the office for Lauren. Instead she begins each day by walking her very helpful assistant, Felix, the miniature poodle. When they return home, she makes a large mug of tea, turns on the radio and spends the majority of the day working in her home studio.

There will be emails to answer and orders to process, as well as working hard on her new shop website that will be launching very soon alongside her existing Etsy shop. As an internet based business it's really important to keep up to date with social media, as well as blogging regularly to

keep in touch with online customers. Lauren tells us that she absolutely loves Pinterest and takes frequent breaks to browse for party inspiration and trends, as well as uploading her own content. At present Lauren's developing a new wedding stationery range so there's lots of sketching and pattern development happening in her studio, as well as working on her cake toppers which are becoming very popular. And if it all gets just a little too hectic, then there's always crochet waiting and the chance to hook up something beautiful!

We asked Lauren what advice she'd give to others hoping to start their own businesses. Her unequivocal response was that you must offer something unique, be prepared to work incredibly hard and be passionate about what you're doing. Running your own business is very different to having a 9-5 job in that you alone are responsible for every part of your business, so need to be self-motivated and carry out a lot of forward planning. It's so easy to concentrate on just the bits you enjoy, but you mustn't neglect the administrative side either – it's really important to keep on top of everything and you can always make it more enjoyable by using lovely stationery! Be prepared for the shock of working alone if you've always worked alongside others. It's easy to feel isolated and you have to make the effort to socialise. Lauren runs a local crochet group and attends talks and workshops where she can meet other like-minded people.

Sometime in the future Lauren's dream is to open a physical party shop alongside her online business, but most of all she hopes to carry on growing Paper Doily Party Shop through her hard work, patience and perseverance.

Be sure to pop over to Lauren's shop
www.etsy.com/uk/shop/PaperDoilyPart
yShop

Look!
a lovely idea
- - - - - - - - - - - - - - -
Woven Wall
Hanging

Looking for a way to use up all your leftover
yarn scraps? Then look no further! Make this
gorgeous woven wall hanging with a fab tutorial
by Francesca from Fall For DIY.

Image & Tutorial: www.fallfordiy.com

BUSTLE & SEW

LOVE TO SEW AND SEW WITH LOVE

Flora the Prettiest Puppy

With her head cocked enquiringly to one side and two black beady eyes looking up at you, Flora really is the prettiest little puppy and sure to be a great favourite with children and the young at heart everywhere.

Flora is adapted from a vintange - mid 20th century - Italian pattern. I've just made a few adjustments to her gusset so she will stand better without her legs slipping out sideways and also shortened and reshaped her ears.

Flora stands a petite, but very pretty, 5" tall (approx)

Materials

- FQ or less printed cotton fabric (non-stretchy)

- 9" square felt

- Two small black spherical beads

- ¼" button for nose

- Scrap of printed cotton fabric or narrow ribbon for collar

- Decorative button for collar

- Stranded cotton embroidery floss or perle thread

- Toy stuffing

- Stuffing stick - this is easy to make and is really helpful for stuffing narrow parts of the body. Just break the point off a bamboo skewer and fray the end so it "grabs" the stuffing as you work with it.

Method

Flora is so very easy to make you almost don't need any instructions! Which is just as well since although I learned Latin at school that was a very long time ago - and wasn't really much help when looking at the vintage pattern - which is written in Italian!

- Cut out all pieces using the full size template.

- You can make Flora entirely from felt in which case omit the next step ...... Machine zig zag all around the edge of the two body shapes, the tail and the head gusset. This will prevent excessive fraying.

- Join all pieces with wrong sides together using cross stitch and three strands of cotton floss. I chose a nice bright blue that would contrast prettily with my taupe gingham check fabric. To stitch the seams first work one direction in half-cross stitch, then return in the other direction to complete the stitch. This makes a nice strong seam that won't come unravelled if one stitch is broken.

- First join the gussets to the body pieces around the ends of the legs.

- Sew gusset pieces together along centre seam.

- Place on fabric and one felt ear shape wrong sides together and stitch all around the edge in cross stitch as before.

- Stitch around the nose and attach the head gusset, inserting the ears into the seam a the top of the head (see photo for guide to positioning). The more curved edge of the ear should be at the front of the softie.

- Fold the tail piece in half lengthways, matching at c. Stuff, using your stuffing

stick to push the stuffing well up into the tip of the tail.

- Sew up body from tops of gussets to D inserting tail as indicated.

- Stuff your toy firmly - remember stuffing will compact with time so it's best to over stuff a little - though not too much - you don't want to distort the shape or put stress on the seams.

- Close the top of the body, adding more stuffing as you go so the body remains firm - particularly at the narrowest point of the abdomen.

- Use glass-headed pins to mark the position of the eyes. Take your time over this as their positioning will affect the final expression of your softie. When you're happy stitch the black beads into place taking your thread right through the head and pulling firmly to create eye sockets for the beads to sit in.

- Stitch small button to tip of nose.

- Wrap fabric strip or ribbon around neck and secure at the front with decorative button.

- Flora is now finished.

May's Favourite Blogs

Feeling Stitchy is written by a diverse group of volunteer craft bloggers who contribute weekly, monthly, or from time to time.

Madalynne's blog is both useful and beautiful, providing lessons and tutorials on pattern making and sewing

All things quilty in a fresh, vibrant, colourful format - the clue's in the name over at Red Pepper Quilts!

Crochet Nirvana is a place where Robin shares her adventures in learning crochet and learning in life.

HARD is the

Heart

THAT

Loves naught in

MAY

Geoffrey Chaucer

MAY/2015

MO	TU	WE	TH	FR	SA	SU
				1	2	3
4	5	6	7	8	9	10
11	12	13	14	15	16	17
18	19	20	21	22	23	24
25	26	27	28	29	30	31

And finally ... it's time for Tea and Trivia .....

Everything's coming up ... hawthorn!

Hawthorn is also known as mayflower. The saying 'Ne'er cast a clout 'til May is out' may refer to the flowering of the hawthorn, or it may refer to the month of May. Either way it's time to put away winter clothing!

GOING STRAIGHT

Need to cut your fabric straight across? Instead of tearing it, snip into the selvedge on one side and then pull out a thread from the snipped area. Tug on it gently and pull the thread away from the fabric. This will cause some gathering as you push the fabric. Continue right across whole width. Once you've removed the thread, cut along the line that's left by the space where the thread used to be and you will have cut a straight line across the grain.

All pinned up!

When pinning a seam for machine stitching, place your pins at right-angles to the stitching line. Then if your needle does hit a pin it will simply slide off to form the stitch rather than breaking. (99% of the time anyway!)

The Darling Buds of May

Is line from one of Shakespeare's sonnets. Later used as a book title by H E Bates, it was turned into a British comedy drama series in the 1990s that helped to launch Catherine Zeta-Jones' career.

Mayday

The word mayday is internationally recognised as a distress call. Its use originated in 1923 by Frederick Stanley Mockford (1897–1962). A senior radio officer at Croydon Airport in London, Mockford was asked to think of a word that would indicate distress and would easily be understood by all pilots and ground staff in an emergency.

Canterbury Tales

May is a character in the Merchant's Tale part of Geoffrey Chaucer's Canterbury Tales. May was young woman who married a 60 year-old knight Januarie. The name is thought to represent youth opposing her husband's old age.

Woolly jumpers!

No, not spring lambs - just time to put away your winter clothes. Do be careful with the use of mothballs. Many children and pets are naturally attracted to them with deadly results. Another option would be cedar blocks or cedar lined storage. Mothballs and cedar can be effective against insects, but keep in mind that neither is a complete guarantee. Just like with other cleaning products, storage chemicals should be used with care and according to directions.

Shall I compare thee to a summer's day? Thou art more lovely and more temperate: Rough winds do shake the darling buds of May. And summer's lease hath all too short a date.

Sonnet 18, Wm Shakespeare

Conversion Tables

Volume

Imperial	Metric
2 fl oz	55 ml
3 fl oz	75 ml
5 fl oz (¼ pint)	150 ml
10 fl oz (½ pint)	275 ml
1 pint	570 ml
1 ¼ pint	725 ml
1 ¾ pint	1 litre
2 pint	1.2 litre
2½ pint	1.5 litre
4 pint	2.25 litres

Weights

Imperial	Metric
½ oz	10 g
¾ oz	20 g
1 oz	25 g
1½ oz	40 g
2 oz	50 g
2½ oz	60 g
3 oz	75 g
4 oz	110 g
4½ oz	125 g
5 oz	150 g
6 oz	175 g
7 oz	200 g
8 oz	225 g
9 oz	250 g
10 oz	275 g
12 oz	350 g
1 lb	450 g

Oven Temperatures

Gas Mark	°F	°C
1	275°F	140°C
2	300°F	150°C
3	325°F	170°C
4	350°F	180°C
5	375°F	190°C
6	400°F	200°C
7	425°F	220°C
8	450°F	230°C
9	475°F	240°C

American Cup Conversions

American	Imperial	Metric
1 cup flour	5oz	150g
1 cup caster/granulated sugar	8oz	225g
1 cup brown sugar	6oz	175g
1 cup butter/margarine/lard	8oz	225g
1 cup sultanas/raisins	7oz	200g
1 cup currants	5oz	150g
1 cup ground almonds	4oz	110g
1 cup golden syrup	12oz	350g
1 cup uncooked rice	7oz	200g
1 cup grated cheese	4oz	110g
1 stick butter	4oz	110g

Liquid Conversions

Imperial	Metric	American
½ fl oz	15 ml	1 tbsp
1 fl oz	30 ml	1/8 cup
2 fl oz	60 ml	¼ cup
4 fl oz	120 ml	½ cup
8 fl oz	240 ml	1 cup
16 fl oz	480 ml	1 pint

Note: A pint isn't always a pint: in British, Australian and often Canadian recipes you'll see an imperial pint listed as 20 fluid ounces. American and some Canadian recipes use the the American pint measurement, which is 16 fluid ounces.

Templates

Template

Full size and with choice of alternative texts

Welcome

Craft Room

Studio

Our Home

Pin Cushion Template

Full size and reversed to suit your
preferred method of transfer.

Mr Toad
Template

Full size

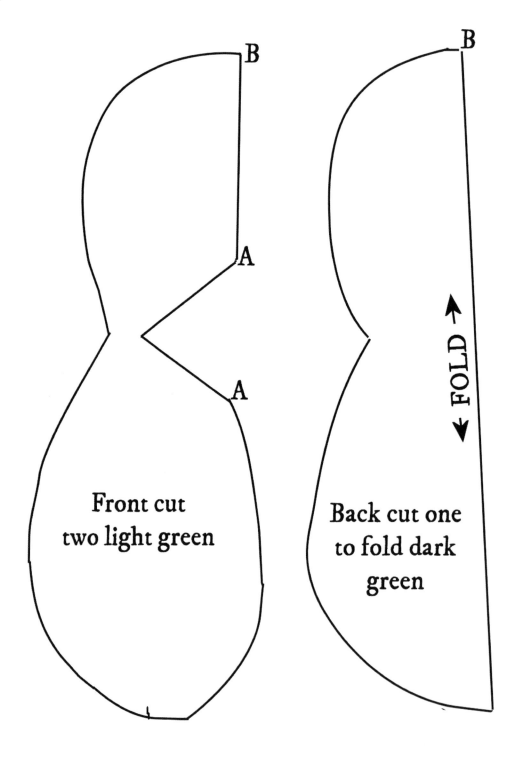

B

B

A

A

FOLD

Front cut
two light green

Back cut one
to fold dark
green

Cut 2 arms in light and 2 in dark green
Cut 2 legs in light and 2 in dark green

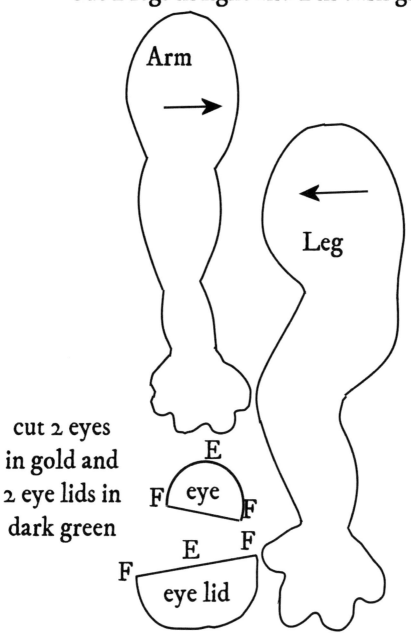

Arm

Leg

cut 2 eyes
in gold and
2 eye lids in
dark green

E

F eye F

E F

F

eye lid

Gardener's Apron Template

Full size.

Comfortable Cushion Template

Text is full size and also reversed to suit your preferred method of transfer. The flowers are reversed to trace onto the paper side of your Bondaweb. The small picture is for ease of reference when joining your templates together.

Are you sitting Comfortably?

Are you sitting Comfort ably?

Are you
sitting
Comfort
ably?

Flora the prettiest Puppy

Full size.

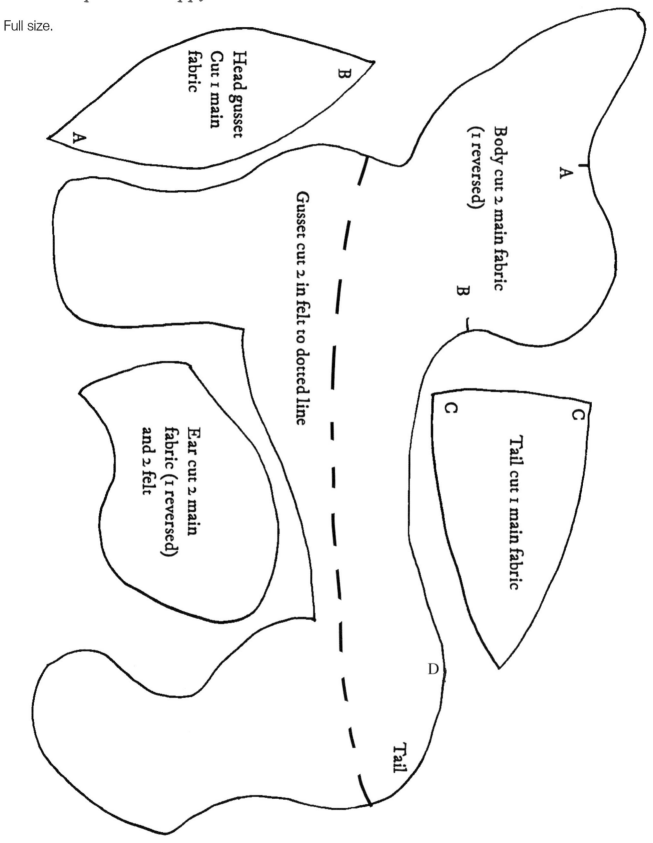

Head gusset
Cut 1 main
fabric

Body cut 2 main fabric
(1 reversed)

Gusset cut 2 in felt to dotted line

Ear cut 2 main
fabric (1 reversed)
and 2 felt

Tail cut 1 main fabric

Tail

11666041R00037

Printed in Great Britain
by Amazon.co.uk, Ltd.,
Marston Gate.